Songs of the Heart

Poems by Daniel Wright

Copyright © 2022, Daniel Wright

I See

I see Christian's but no Christ.

I see humans but no humanity.

I see hunger but everybody's full.

I see poverty but everybody's rich.

The pastor lives in a mansion but Christ lives on the street.

The morning is started with bombs and bullets.

Darkened hearts and selfish minds lead the way.

To be rich your heart must die.

Power corrupts and money corrupts absolutely.

What was that quote? "It is easier for a camel to go through the

Eye of a needle than it is for a rich man to enter heaven."

Selfishness and greediness are not the gifts of the spirit,

But rather the gifts of the enemy.

Hymn to love

Love
Bled for us
Love cried for us
Love died for us
Forgive
Accept
And love each other
The words He spoke
He is the good shepherd
I've died into you
My old self is gone
I am a new creation

You are my love
Both now and forever
I need no one else
I and you
Forevermore
In blissful unity
To walk with you
In Heaven
All the days of my life

Amen.

The Butterfly

Flying
Flying up and down
Wings as soft
As water
The butterfly
Gods grace personified.

Does God Cry?

Does God Cry
When good people
Die
Are his tears the rain
Are the clouds
In the sky
From Heaven
And are they
Too sweet for
This World?

Does He love
Them so much
That He brings
Immediately to Heaven

Are the pure
Heart so close
To god that
He cries when
they are hurt?

Surely the purest
And most loving
Heart cries when
All His Creation
Is in pain
But I ask
Does God cry
When good oeople
Die?

The Peaceful Mind

Still, like a pond
Silent, like a mountaintop
Strong, like a fortified wall
Simple, like nature.

Silence

I sit here
In my cell
My heart pumping
I feel my lungs
Fill with air.
Your spirit
Fills my body
My mind is quieted
All I know is you.
I feel the bliss of
Sanctification enter my being
I am made holy.
I love you
I know you.
Silence.

Begga Love

When I see
Love I see a
Beggar
When I see a
Beggar I see Christ
When I see Christ
I see Love
When I see Love
I see God.

Why are we so
Hard on ourselves
When deep inside
We all have the
Seed of warmth
In our hearts

I love you
With all my heart
May Love fall on you
Like rain from a storm cloud
I Love you
Go in peace.

What if Christ came back

Preaching unity and love
What if Christ came back
As pure as a dove
Trying to stop the division
As we are all one
Imagine the bliss
Put down the gun
A single mother
Dad not in the picture
Immigrant stepfather
Poor and humble
What if Christ came back
And the world would be as one.

Crying over you

I am dead
Inside and out
I don't see
Joy anymore
Love for me is dead

I don't want you
I don't need you
You are happy
Life is grey
Crying over you

You have thrown
Me in the gutter
No longer shall I
See your smile

We are done
Darkness has corroded
My light
You don't care
I don't care
I am here
Crying over you

If I jumped
Off a bridge
I would be
Free
Maybe a smile
On my face
As I hit
The water
I am free.

Yeshua

In my heartbeat
I feel you
When the robin chirps
I hear your love
When the sun rises
I see your light
When I sip water
I taste your spirit
When the rain falls
And the earth releases her sweat
I smell your fragrance.
Amen.

My heart opens
Like a flower

Red roses
Yellow roses
Love
Fire
Passion
And
Romance
My
Heart
Opens
Like
Love
On
Fire.

Hymn to Odin

O Hanged Man
Hung on the tree
For Nine days
Learnin' the runes
And the magic thereof
Pierced by a spear
And hung by your foot
You grew in your
Wisdom by drinking
From Mimir's well
Cutting out your eye
And drinking the mead
Became the words that
Grew the world of Midgard
With Frigg by your side
Thor came into being
Your son the lover
Of mankind, to you
Three we pay homage.

Let me rise, Lord

Let me rise, Lord
In your eyes
Let me rise
In your arms
Let me rise
In your thoughts
Let me rise
I have abandoned thee
And seek to do forgiveness

So let me rise, Lord
In your favor
Let me rise
In your light
Let me rise
In your Love
Let me rise
For I have abandoned
The flock
And seek to return

I am sick
Of my sin
Misery pain and death
Do I feel
I wish to see your light
And feel your warmth
So let me rise

Let me rise, Lord
Open my heart
Let me rise
Enlighten my soul
Let me rise
Awaken my spirit
Let me rise
Save me from death
I want life
Let me rise.

The Long Sleep

Death Death Death
Sleeping forever
I'm finally free
Tho I do long
For that lifeless hand
Her gentle touch on my shoulder
I can finally exhale
I am at peace
For the first time
Just let me sleep.

Emily

A school
Rustburg
Did I love it
No
Did I love her
Yes
She never hated me
Not that I know
She's probably forgotten me
But I remember her

Hair as blonde
As the sun
Eyes shining like
Angels
She never put me down
Emily

I'd track her
Down if I could
Pages through the
Years and her picture in
The yearbook

I don't know if
I'll ever see her again
Maybe
I don't know
One day
Deep down
I hope.

Emily.

Separation

God is in everything
In the trees
In the leaves
In the wood
In the bark
In the dirt
In the soil
In the roots
In the water
In the bugs
In the bones
In the flesh
In the blood
In the veins
In the muscles
In the tissue
In the fat
In the organs
In the brains
In the hair
In the teeth
In the eyes
In the eyelashes
In the eyebrows
In the waste
In the gases
In the vomit
In the bile
In the spit
In the rocks
In the stones
In the boulders
In the grass
In the weeds
In the plants
In the flowers
In the crops
In the birds
In the cats
In the dogs
In the lizards
In the reptiles
In the scales
In the gills
In the fish
In the squids
In the octopus
In the coral
In the lava
In the plankton
In the whales
In the atoms
In the electrons
In the protons
In the sound waves
In the speed of light
In the speed of dark
In the speed of sound
In the planets
In the stars
In the dark matter
In the black holes
In the light matter
In the asteroids
In the meteors
In the rain
In the thunder
In the lightning
In the snow
In the ice
In the fire
In the smoke
In the lava
In the magma
God is in everything
So why the lies of separation

Cold silent night

Cold, freezing, nearly dead
Snow building upon I
Alone. Dark grey sky
Visibility zero
I reach out
Anyone there?

My bones are stiffening
My blood is calming
I feel like giving up
Shall I die here alone?

Mountains are my
Surrounding tomb
No cabin with a
Welcoming fire
No company
No voices of loved ones
No soft comfort
Does God even acknowledge I?

I am surely dead
To the world
If mine own family
Doth forget me
I shall die in my
Slumber

Lest at last
I look up
And see light
As if the gates
Of the heavens
Calling unto I

I raise up
There is a village
My flare
One alone and final
I shoot it up into the sky

Finally I see compassion
Doth the lord then
Forgive me?

I am at peace
I have found my love
Warm fire
A soft bed
A loving dog and family

I
Am
At
Peace.

Whirling Love

You set life into motion
You set love on fire
O sweet lord of fiery love
I am wrapped up in your fire
So, drunk with your love
Whirling around like a drunken fool
I no longer feel misery
I am so yours forever
My sweet love
I love you so much.

Your eyes are so beautiful
My illusions are shattered
Your beautiful amazing
Golden fiery face
Nothing but pure love
Your heart is in mine and mine in yours
You are the ocean
And I am the raindrop
My sweet beautiful lord
Loving bliss, is your name
Wherever couples are intwined,
The musk is your scent.

I dance for you
My romantic king
You are pure
So pure.
So radiant
My mind is speechless
But my heart is burning with
Your praise,
Kiss me
I will kiss you back
Passionate,
Maddening love
So, warmed by your grace
I say to my family,
Come and sit by the fire
And wrap yourself in its light.

My sweet, passionate, radiant lord.
I am yours,
Forever.

I

I am
I am the all
I dissolve myself into
Everything
And become nothing

Nothingness at one
With reality
Simplicity and bliss
I am
I am
I am

At once I dissolve
To be at this time
My true universal
Self
Totally divine
I am
I am
I am.

Tiny little knives

Tiny little knives
Pierce my heart
It begins to bleed
Red tears of sorrow

I fall down and sigh
Last one alive
This pain is scorching
I feel like a maniac
Tiny little knives

Death came to me this
Morning
I felt his cold grip
Freedom at last

Why can't I just
Smile
Laugh and be cheery
It's my lot in life
Dead inside and out
I am nothingness

I am pierced
By tiny little knives.

Pluto

Alone
Falling ashes
Night with no moon
Nor sun
Cold and dead
Call out to
See if any one
Heard me

No one says
A word
All I hear is
Freezing cold wind
I walk on ice
Sound of chaos
Swirls around me

No one cares
No one hears
No one loves
No one sees

I am alone
In this void of death
Black sky's and

No joy
How I miss her
And no one cares

Ice and death
Surround me
I walk but
No one sees
I am invisible

Guess I'll just
Lay here and
Die

Is God even here?
Dark nihilism is
All I feel
Empty inside
I accept death

Joy has overcome me
I am now at one
With the angels.

Hallelujah

A dead heart and a foul mind

A child
No love
Felt inside
Or outside
A mind full of ignorance
A heart full of hate
I want this life to end

Every night
I wish for death
Every morning
Is a disappointment
To feel that cold icy grip
Would be paradise
For me.

Cold venomous people
Speech as deadly as knives
Every day
All day
8-3
Damn this place
I am alone
Crying in the darkness
Is anybody out there?

The lover and the beloved

Dancing, whirling, singing
All in your name
My love
I'd travel to the ends of
The earth for you.
Your light in my spirit
Your love in my heart
I burn for your sake
My sweet beloved
Everywhere I look
I see your face
Beautiful and radiant light.

Sing to me
And joy will wash over my
Heart. I cry at night
Wanting to see you
My sweet beloved
I am on fire for your being
Everyone has your name
Everyone has your face.

You are one
And one in all
All is you
You are all
Everyone and everything
Is a mirror for you
And by you
Yet I am alone
And I long for your touch
My sweet romantic spirit
Fiery passionate friend
Possess me so that I may
Feel you. Enrapture me in
Your sweat.
The butterfly and the
Hummingbird, are your light.

My beloved
You are here
And I am you
And you are me
My eyes open
And I am in bliss
I love you
My sweet passionate friend.

Whirl

I wish I could whirl
I wish I could whirl
Whirl around you forever
Forever intoxicated by your love
Your blissful light raining down on the world
I could sing your names forever
I don't care if my home would be a cave in the mountains
I know you are everywhere
I love you
And you are my beloved
One day when my body shuts
Ill finally see your face
And fall in love with LOVE

I Survived

Joker
One kid
A few many schools
Some rather worse
Some mild
The masters did nothing
The overseers did nothing
Yet I survived
Fights
Bullying
Vocal threats
Yet I survived
Name calling
Snickering
Suicidal thoughts
Yet I survived
I am a warrior
I'm a survivor
I'm not a failure
I have survived.

Social Introvert

I love it
Quite
Solitude
I've always hated
Crowds

Misanthrope?
No
I prefer to be
Alone
As soon as I'm
Not alone
I can't wait to
Be alone

Do I miss people
Of course I do
Is it miserable though
I love it
I don't mind going

To the cinema
I don't mind
Going to concerts
Plays, restaurants, bars

At home
I'm alone
But I'm not
I love the quiet
I love the peace

If I could be
A hermit
I would do it
In a heartbeat
To be amongst
The trees
To hear the wind
In the trees
Nothing but life.

Jelly Bean

I look at her
My heart swells up
I love you
Forever.

About the Author

Daniel is a poet from Lynchburg Virginia who through his life has been influenced by many spiritual and mystical paths. He has since been compelled to write spiritual poetry and poetry about everyday goings on.

www.ingramcontent.com/pod-product-compliance
Lightning Source LLC
Chambersburg PA
CBHW040723060526

44119CB00083B/301